CAREERS THAT SAVE LIVES

PARAMEDIC

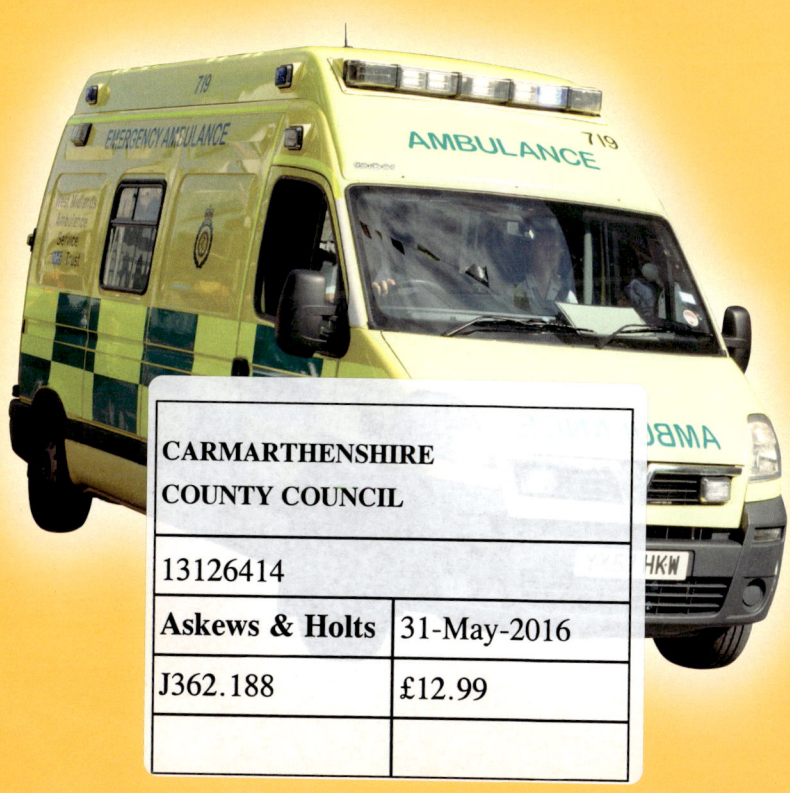

Louise Spilsbury

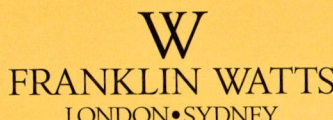

FRANKLIN WATTS
LONDON • SYDNEY

Franklin Watts
First published in Great Britain in 2016 by The Watts Publishing Group

Credits
Series Editors: Sarah Eason and Jennifer Sanderson
Series Designer: Emma DeBanks

Picture credits: Cover: Shutterstock: Corepics VOF (top), London Ambulance Service
NHS Trust (bottom); Inside: Dreamstime: Aprescindere 25t, CandyBox Images
10, 13, Flynt 11, Wellphotos 25b, Michael Zhang 19; Shutterstock: 1000 Words
15, 18, CandyBox Images 4–5, 7, 14, 16–17, Gcpics 4, Brendan Howard 22–23,
I4lcocl2 20–21, Jan Kranendonk 20, Laurens Parsons Photography 9, Lars Lindblad
2, 8, 26, Lucian Milasan 1, 6, 28, Volt Collection 27.

Dewey number: 362.1'88
ISBN: 978 1 4451 4509 9

Printed in China

MIX
Paper from
responsible sources
FSC® C104740

Franklin Watts
An imprint of
Hachette Children's Group
Part of The Watts Publishing Group
Carmelite House
50 Victoria Embankment
London EC4Y 0DZ

An Hachette UK Company
www.hachette.co.uk

www.franklinwatts.co.uk

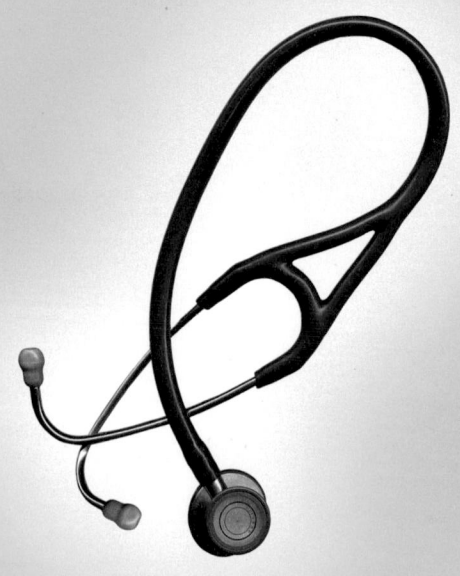

CONTENTS

SAVING LIVES

When people are choosing a career, what do you think matters most to them? Do you think how well a job pays is important to many people? Some people want a job that is interesting and pays well but more than anything, they want to do something that makes a positive contribution to the world. Careers that really count are those that make a difference in other people's lives. These are jobs in the **public service** and include police officers, aid workers and firefighters.

Serving the Public

Public-service careers not only make a difference to other people's lives but the people who do them also get a lot of satisfaction from their work. The jobs can be challenging, difficult and sometimes even dangerous. However, the people who do them are happy in their chosen careers because they enjoy being able to use their knowledge, skills and expertise to help others. Some people work to save lives, investigate crimes or rescue people from danger. In this book we will look at the work of paramedics.

When there is a medical emergency, paramedics are ready to help.

A Career for You?

Here are three things you can do to work out if a career that counts might be right for you.

- Know what you are good at doing. Think about what you like doing and what other people say you are good at.
- Know what type of work setting you like. Do you enjoy being outdoors or at a desk? Do you like to work with people or do you prefer working alone?
- Find out about your chosen job and what it is really like. Reading this book is a good place to start.

HEROES ON THE MOVE

Paramedics do an incredibly important job. They give people immediate medical care before they can be taken to a hospital. Paramedics are often the first to arrive at the scene of accidents, medical emergencies and **natural disasters**. They give medical treatment to the victims of car crashes, to people hurt in natural disasters and people who have suffered a medical emergency at home. Paramedics perform life-saving treatments on patients to make sure they are **stable** before they are taken to a hospital.

WHAT MAKES A GREAT PARAMEDIC?

Paramedics complete a course and follow an **intensive** training programme to be certain they have all the skills they need for the job. However, there are also some important **characteristics** all paramedics need. They must be:
- Quick thinking: paramedics need to be able to quickly make decisions in difficult situations.
- Calm: paramedics need to keep calm when everyone around them may be panicking.
- Caring: paramedics must have a strong desire to help people.

Which of the above do you think is most important and why?

To save lives, paramedics have to stay calm and act quickly.

Becoming a Paramedic

There are some basic requirements that all paramedics must have before starting their career. They must be at least 18 years old. In the UK, you must have a minimum of five GCSEs and two A levels before completing a paramedic science degree course or a diploma. Different regions in Australia have different entry requirements, so make sure you check websites carefully before applying. Applicants around the world will also need a full driver's licence and complete training on the job.

A TYPICAL DAY

There is no such thing as a typical day for a paramedic! The number and types of calls vary each day. Paramedics in the UK can work for the National Health Service (NHS) but others in the UK and around the world may choose to work for a private company. Here, we look at the kind of things paramedics might be called on to do over a day and a night.

PARAMEDICS' DAY

- **Midnight** At the start of a shift, paramedics check their ambulance. They complete a checklist to be sure that all their equipment is working, enough supplies are on hand and the vehicle is ready.
- **2 am** Paramedics get some sleep.
- **4:45 am** There is a call to an elderly man who has collapsed at his home. Paramedics examine him and then take him to hospital.
- **6 am** Breakfast time.
- **7 am** Paramedics complete chores such as cleaning the ambulance.
- **9 am** A call to a nursing home is answered. A patient is ill and must be transferred to a hospital.
- **11 am** Another call is received, this time to a car accident. The victim is treated and taken to a hospital.
- **4 pm** Paramedics rest or watch television. They also spend time on the computer, taking courses to keep their skills up to date.
- **10 pm** A call comes in. It is to a nightclub where there has been a fight. Paramedics drive to the incident.
- **Midnight** The shift ends.

Every day is different for paramedics, so they must be prepared for all kinds of emergencies.

Every Day is Different

Some shifts may have very few calls, while others may have so many that the paramedic does not return to the ambulance station. Emergency services function 24 hours a day, so a paramedic has irregular working hours.

RESPONDING TO CALLS

In an emergency, people dial 999 and speak to an operator. The operator then **dispatches** paramedics (and sometimes other emergency services) to the scene. Paramedics answer calls to assist people in need every day. Emergency calls are urgent. People may be seriously ill and in need of urgent help. Responding to calls quickly and **efficiently** is vital for paramedics.

Paramedics always wear their uniforms while they are on duty, so that when called to an emergency, they can race straight to their ambulance. They must drive very quickly to an emergency, so they turn on the ambulance's sirens and lights to warn drivers and pedestrians that they need to move out of the way. Ambulance drivers can go through red lights if necessary, as long as they do not put anyone in danger.

A paramedic team must respond quickly to a call for help.

Knowing the Area

Paramedics must take time to get to know the names of all the streets and major landmarks or buildings in their local area. This helps them to respond to emergency calls quickly and efficiently.

WHAT MAKES A GREAT PARAMEDIC?

Paramedics need to have a strong **work ethic**, which is a belief in the value and importance of hard work. They often have to respond to a lot of emergencies in a single day, at all hours and even during holidays. How do you think having a strong work ethic helps paramedics to handle the demands of their job?

Ambulances have flashing lights and sirens to keep the public safe and help the paramedics to get to an emergency swiftly.

IN THE AMBULANCE

Paramedics do not always spend a lot of time at the ambulance station. On some shifts, they mainly work from their ambulance so that they can remain **mobile** and travel to people who are in need. Paramedics carry all the equipment they need to give people immediate medical assistance in the ambulance.

Here is some of the life-saving equipment that can be found inside an ambulance:

- Heart **monitors** and **defibrillators** – used to check patients with heart problems.
- Medical kits – carry supplies used to treat patients.
- **Stretchers** and boards – used to move patients.
- **Oxygen tanks** – used to treat patients who have breathing problems.
- **Splints** – used to treat broken arms and legs.
- **Spinal collars** – hold the head and neck still. These are used if paramedics are concerned that the patient may have back or neck injuries.
- A **blood pressure** cuff – allows paramedics to measure and record a person's blood pressure.

WHAT MAKES A GREAT PARAMEDIC?

Paramedics respond quickly to a call. They must drive the ambulance speedily to an emergency, and choose the equipment needed to treat patients. Paramedics must stay calm and collected at all times. How do you think keeping calm when travelling to an **incident** and assisting people can help paramedics to do their job?

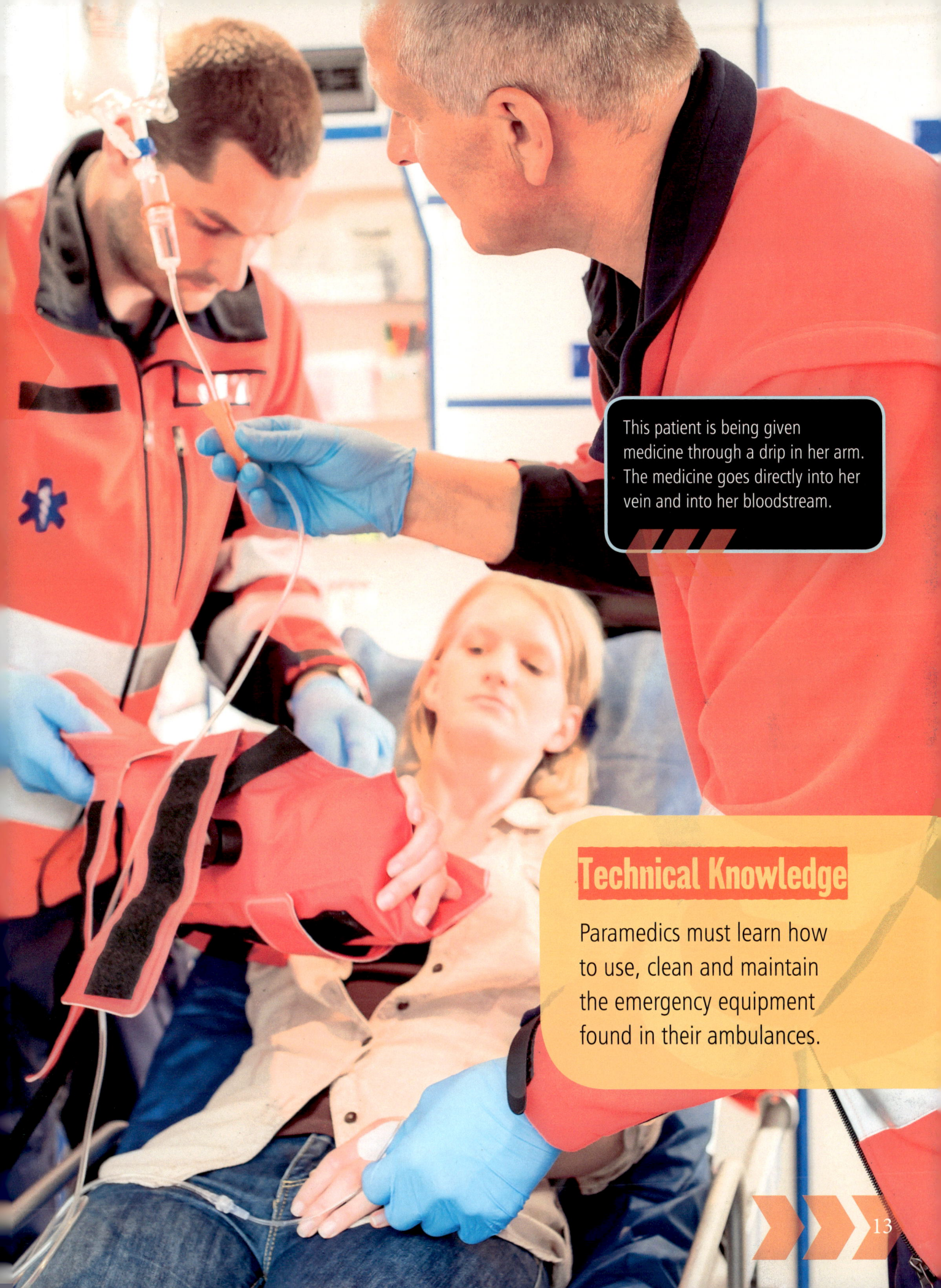

This patient is being given medicine through a drip in her arm. The medicine goes directly into her vein and into her bloodstream.

Technical Knowledge

Paramedics must learn how to use, clean and maintain the emergency equipment found in their ambulances.

EXAMINING PATIENTS

As soon as the paramedics arrive at the scene of an accident or another medical emergency, they must examine a patient carefully to work out what immediate help is needed. It is important to make the patient stable so that he or she can be transported to a hospital, where medical attention can be given.

Paramedics must check if the patient is having trouble breathing. They must note if the patient is bleeding. If the patient is awake, the paramedic can ask him or her questions about what happened and about any medication being taken or medical history the paramedic may need to know about. If the patient is not **conscious**, paramedics question those who are present at the scene. Along with the physical examination, this helps the paramedic to decide what is wrong and what action to take next.

Knowing what piece of equipment to use when treating a patient is often a matter of life and death.

Training Procedures

Paramedics are trained in what **procedures** to follow when examining a patient, so they know what to check first. They will follow medical **protocols** and guidelines. This helps them to check for vital information that is needed to keep a patient safe.

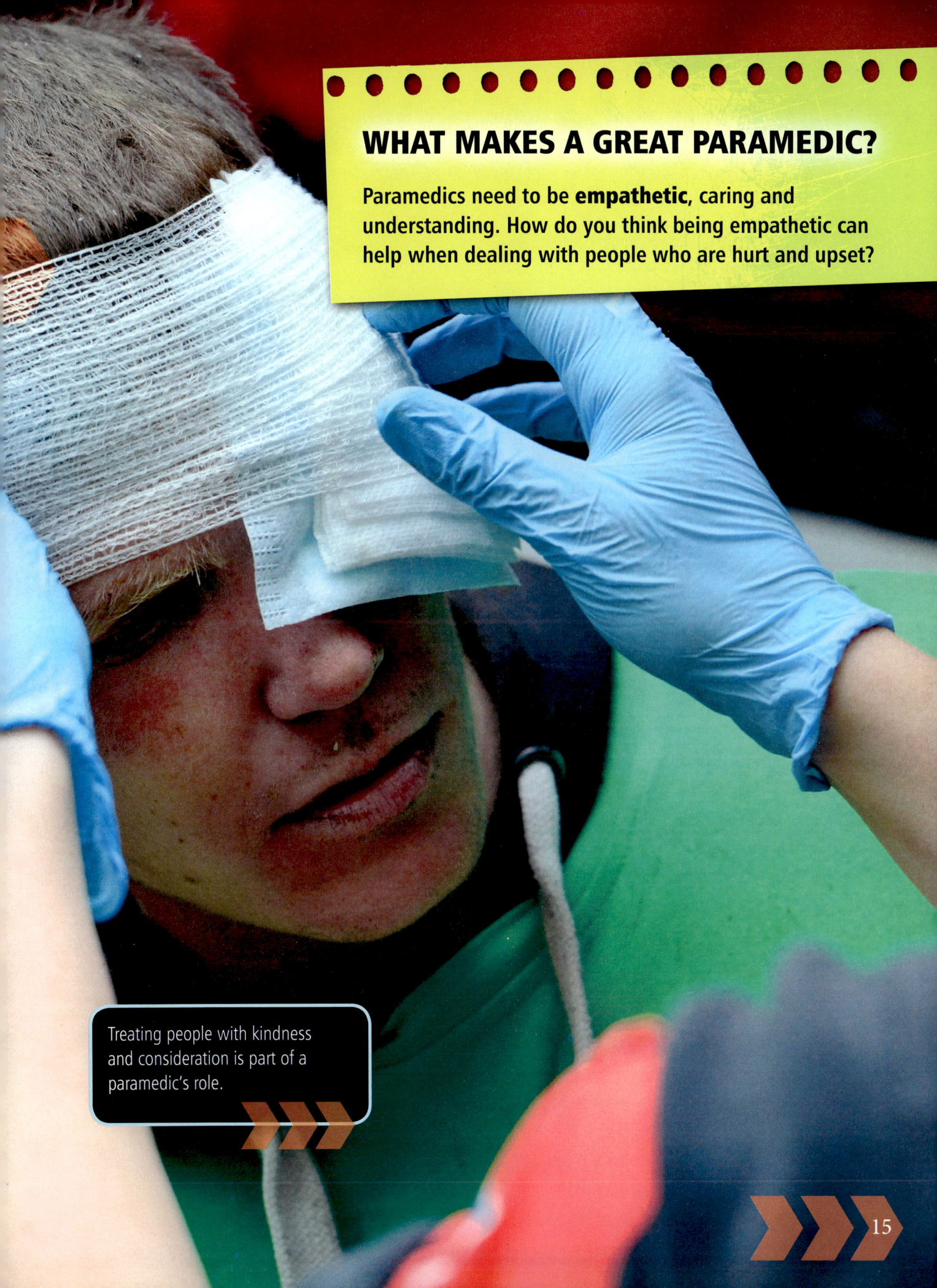

WHAT MAKES A GREAT PARAMEDIC?

Paramedics need to be **empathetic**, caring and understanding. How do you think being empathetic can help when dealing with people who are hurt and upset?

Treating people with kindness and consideration is part of a paramedic's role.

EVERYDAY CARE

Most calls that paramedics attend to may not be as dramatic as those shown on television, but they still are very important. Paramedics must be prepared for anything because they may have to assist in any emergency. They may help a woman to give birth or help someone with severe breathing problems. They may treat someone who is **diabetic** or who has had an **allergic reaction** to a substance.

Paramedics also provide transport for patients from one medical centre or hospital to another. These transfers are common if the paramedics work for private ambulance services. Patients often need to be taken to a hospital that specialises in their injuries or illness. They may need to be transported to a nursing home. Paramedics must often enter people's homes and lift them on to stretchers so they can be taken to a hospital.

WHAT MAKES A GREAT PARAMEDIC?

Paramedics must have good **time-management skills**. They have work to do at the station, scheduled trips to transport patients and they must respond quickly to all emergencies. How do you think having strong time-management skills can help paramedics to do so many jobs quickly and efficiently?

It is important to transport fragile, elderly or ill patients between medical centres with care.

Lifting and Moving

Paramedics are trained to lift and carry patients in a way that does not risk hurting either the patient or themselves. To lift and move people correctly, at least two paramedics must work together. The patient must be carefully strapped to a stretcher and the correct lifting techniques must be used to move him or her.

SAVING LIVES

Paramedics are usually the first people at an emergency scene, and they often take steps that save lives. When called out to an incident, they make decisions and give treatments that keep people alive. They often do so while dealing not only with the patient, but often also with distressed, or aggressive, family members or bystanders.

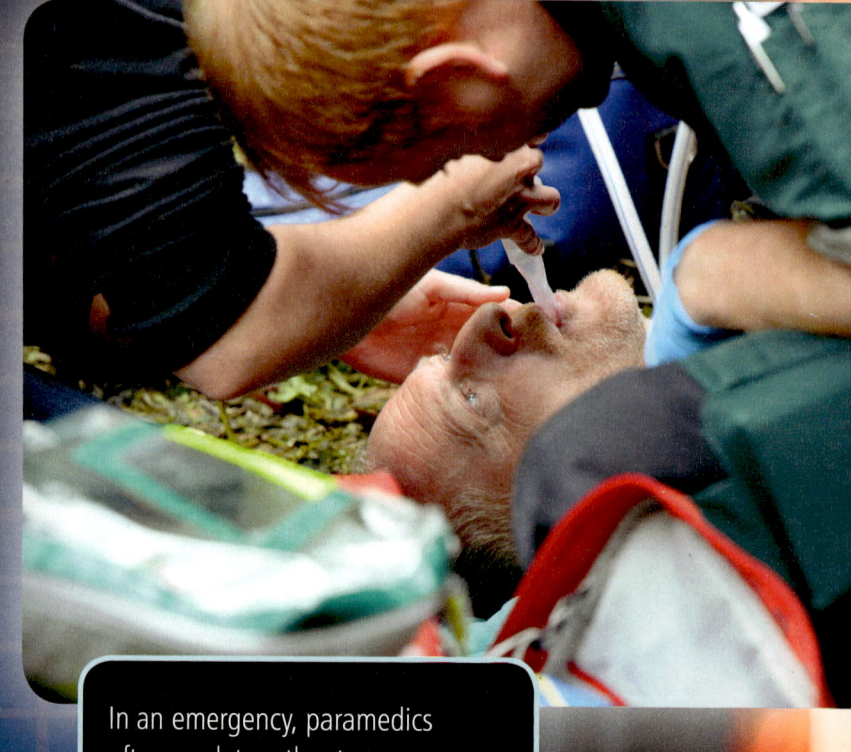

In an emergency, paramedics often work together to save a patient's life.

Gaining Experience

Unlike hospital staff, paramedics must provide life-saving medical care with only the equipment they have in the ambulance. They usually have the help of just one other paramedic, and must work in a great variety of situations. That is why, along with studying techniques in the classroom, inexperienced paramedics also train by working alongside experienced colleagues. This helps them learn how to think and act quickly in response to each situation.

Paramedics often face upsetting situations, such as horrific injuries at a crash scene or a natural disaster. How do you think paramedics prepare themselves to cope with the distressing things they see when they are on duty?

After examining a patient and finding that he or she is in a life-threatening situation, paramedics must decide what action to take. Sometimes this means controlling heavy bleeding, treating **shock** and bandaging wounds. If the patient is not breathing, this may mean tilting the head and clearing the airways of any blockage. The patient's **pulse** is taken to see if the heart is still pumping blood through the **veins**. If there is no pulse, paramedics try to restart the heart, for example, by performing **CPR**.

This paramedic is putting an oxygen mask on a patient to help her to breathe.

19

CRASH SCENES

When paramedics respond to a car accident on the motorway, the scene is likely to be noisy and busy. With traffic quickly passing by, it may also be dangerous. Paramedics have to keep a cool head and assess the situation quickly. In a car crash in which several people may be injured, the paramedics must decide who is in the most urgent need of help and treat them before responding to others.

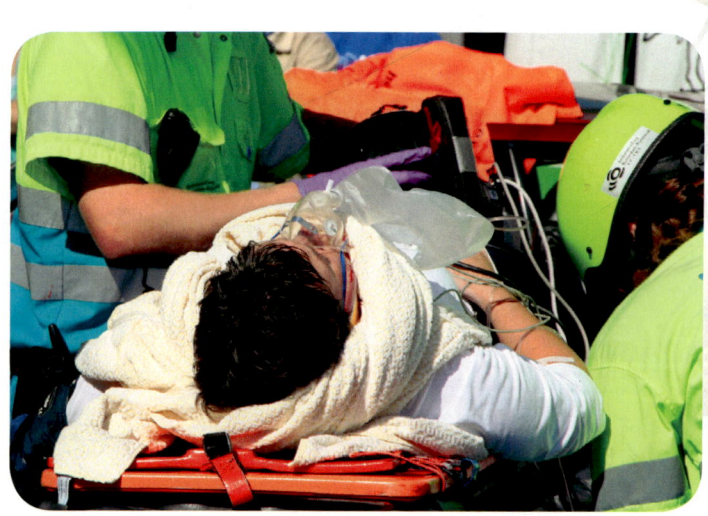

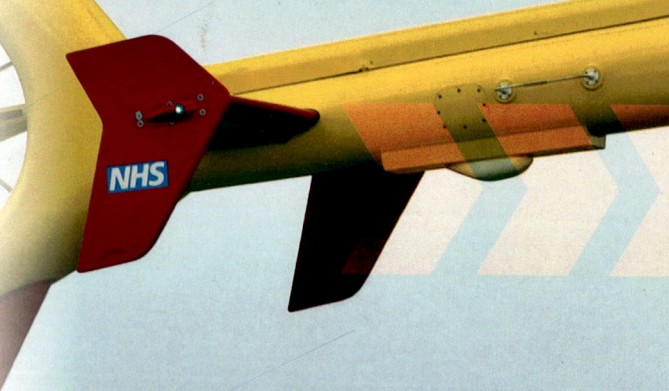

WHAT MAKES A GREAT PARAMEDIC?

Paramedics have to **communicate** with patients, other paramedics, the public and different emergency service workers under stressful situations. How do you think being able to pass on messages quickly and clearly, while also being a good listener and observer, can help paramedics to gather vital information?

Paramedics often have to work with other emergency services at a crash scene. For example, if a victim is trapped in a car, the fire service cuts open the car. While waiting for the firefighters, paramedics examine and treat the victim as best they can. They check **vital signs** and often put on a spinal collar until a back injury is ruled out. Once the victim is removed from the car, the paramedics put him or her on to a **backboard**. The victim is then moved into the ambulance.

Sometimes air ambulances are called to the site of a crash to rush injured people to the nearest hospital for treatment.

Physical Fitness

Paramedics may be required to pull an injured person out of a crushed car or fallen structure. The work is physically demanding because heavy lifting and kneeling are requirements for the job. Paramedics must keep themselves fit and strong in order to carry out their roles.

AT THE HOSPITAL

When paramedics have made sure a patient is stable after an emergency or made someone comfortable after a fall, they drive the patient to a hospital. For example, when a child has broken an arm, the paramedics put a splint around the broken bone, check for shock or other injuries and then take the child to a hospital where the broken bone can be **x-rayed** and set.

On the way to the hospital, paramedics make sure that the patient has no other health problems and that he or she is as comfortable as possible. They watch the patient's blood pressure, heart rate and breathing patterns. At the hospital, paramedics wait with the patient until he or she can be taken to the emergency department. Paramedics tell emergency department staff about the incident, the patient and what actions were taken at the emergency scene. When they leave, paramedics clean the stretcher, replace used supplies in the ambulance and check all the equipment so they are ready for the next call.

Once patients are in safe care at a hospital, ambulances are prepared so they are ready for the next call.

Paperwork

After every call, paramedics have to fill out paperwork. They have to record when and where the incident happened, who was involved, the medical condition and history of the patient and what actions were taken. They also have to make note of what supplies they used and what medication they gave to the patient.

WHAT MAKES A GREAT PARAMEDIC?

Paramedics need to be emotionally stable. That means they need to be caring but not get too upset by other people's distress. How do you think controlling their emotions helps paramedics to deal with life-or-death situations and suffering patients?

TRAINING DAYS

To do their job well, paramedics must have a high level of education and experience. New medical treatments and technologies are being discovered and designed all the time. It is vital that paramedics keep training throughout their career, to make sure they can do their very best for the patients in their care.

A senior paramedic is a more advanced role than a paramedic. They can carry out a wider range of procedures and prescribe a wider range of medications. To do this, senior paramedics have to carry out additional training, often alongside a university or higher education degree. Senior paramedics are often based in GP surgeries, minor injuries units or hospital emergency departments, and they may visit patients in their own homes.

Paramedics learn to do some treatments, such as CPR, on a dummy. Here, a paramedic checks a patient's airways are clear.

WHAT MAKES A GREAT PARAMEDIC?

Paramedics must be motivated. They must really want to do their job well because they have to work hard. They must also keep training to ensure their skills remain up-to-date. How do you think being motivated helps when studying and attending courses to learn new skills?

Before connecting medical equipment to people, paramedics first practise fitting it on to dummies.

Air Ambulance Crew

Some paramedics have extra training to become members of an air ambulance crew. Air ambulance teams fly by helicopter to attend the scene of an accident or emergency in a remote place. Air ambulance paramedics have to learn about navigation, as well as learning about the equipment on a helicopter ambulance.

RISKS AND REWARDS

Working as a paramedic can be tough, both physically and mentally. While on duty, a paramedic is often in personal danger and may have to work with local police in dangerous situations. These include dealing with victims of a traffic accident on a busy road or being called to help someone with gunshot wounds in a dangerous or unsafe area.

As long as a paramedic follows established safety measures, the risks of being injured are greatly reduced and it is rare that a paramedic comes to any harm. The rewards of being a paramedic, on the other hand, are great. Most of the time, a paramedic will enjoy his or her work and, above all, will welcome the opportunity to help others.

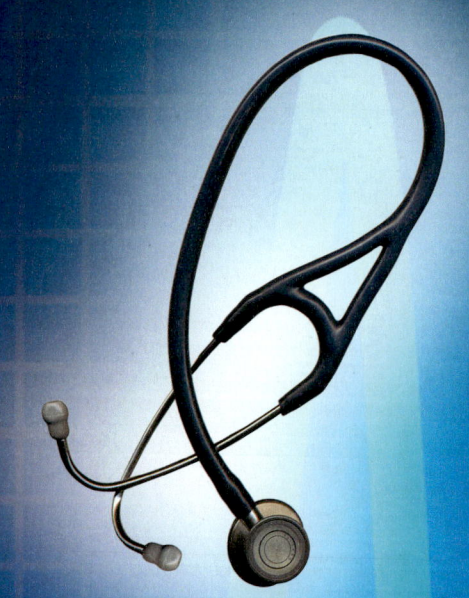

Keeping Safe

Paramedics learn about the science of infections, such as the different types of infections and how they are passed on. This knowledge, and learning how to properly clean and **disinfect** equipment, helps paramedics to keep themselves safe from catching infections while dealing with patients.

At the end of each day, paramedics know that they have done an important job. They know that they have a career that saves lives.

WHAT MAKES A GREAT PARAMEDIC?

Paramedics are not particularly well-paid, and they do not always get the thanks they deserve for the amazing job they do. However, they are **dedicated** and determined people who have a strong desire to help others and do their job to the best of their ability. Could you have the dedication and determination it takes to be a great paramedic?

COULD YOU HAVE A CAREER AS A PARAMEDIC?

Do you want to become a paramedic? These are the steps you will need to take to reach your goal.

Subjects to study at school You will need to study maths or science at school, as well as English. Take opportunities to practise teamwork, too, and to mix and deal with people from a wide range of backgrounds.

Work experience Volunteering at a local hospital can help you to find out what it is like to work in the medical field. It can also help you to practise working and communicating with patients. This kind of volunteer experience may also help a paramedic to stand out when applying for a job.

Exams to pass To become a paramedic you must come away with good grades from school. It might also help to have an interest in maths and science.

University or college There are a number of routes you can take to become a paramedic. Universities offer a paramedic science degree and some institutions or trusts offer diplomas or foundation degrees.

Improve your CV Volunteer in your community. Do not volunteer just to increase your chances of getting a job but because you have a real interest in caring for your fellow citizens. This will also show that you want to care for people in your community.

Life experience Get fit and stay fit. Paramedics need to be physically fit and strong to carry out this demanding job.

Getting the job All paramedics must be at least 18 years old and hold a full driver's licence. Once you have been employed, it is important that all paramedics continue to keep up-to-date with any new medical procedures or technologies that they may use in order to save a patient's life.

GLOSSARY

allergic reaction When someone reacts badly to a usually harmless substance. The person may develop a rash or even stop breathing.

backboard A board used to support a person's back, especially after an accident.

blood pressure The strength of a person's blood pushing against the sides of his or her veins or arteries.

characteristics Features or qualities belonging to a particular person or thing.

communicate To give and receive information.

conscious To be aware of and respond to your surroundings.

CPR An acronym for cardiopulmonary resuscitation. CPR is a first aid technique that can be used if someone is not breathing properly or if his or her heart has stopped.

dedicated Devoted and completely committed to something.

defibrillators Devices that start the heart beating properly again.

diabetic Someone suffering from diabetes, which is a condition that causes a person's blood sugar level to become too high.

disinfect To destroy germs that can cause disease and infections.

dispatches Sends out.

efficiently Well and quickly.

empathetic Having the ability to share another person's feelings.

employers People who pay others to do work.

incident An accident or dangerous event.

intensive Involving a lot of effort or work.

mobile Able to move around easily.

monitors Machines for checking something, such as a person's heart rate.

natural disasters Events such floods, earthquakes and hurricanes that cause great damage or loss of life.

oxygen tanks A means of storing life-saving oxygen that can be given to patients.

procedures Series of actions done in a certain order.

protocols Official ways of doing things.

public service Something that is done to help people rather than to make a profit.

pulse Throbbing that can be felt as blood passes through a major blood vessel, for example, in the wrist.

shift A time period in which different groups of workers do the same jobs in relay.

shock A life-threatening condition that occurs when blood loss stops vital organs, such as the brain and heart, working properly.

spinal collars Devices used to support a patient's neck and head.

splints Strips of hard material used to support broken bones.

stable Not changing.

stretchers Devices used for carrying patients lying down.

time-management skills The ability to plan and control the amount of time a person spends on different tasks to make the most of his or her working day.

vital signs Important body functions, such as breathing and heartbeat.

work ethic A belief in the value and importance of work.

x-rayed Made an image of the inside of the body using an x-ra

FURTHER READING

Ambulance (Emergency 999)
Kathryn Walker, Wayland Books

Ambulance (Emergency Vehicles)
Chris Oxlad, QED Publishing

The Ambulance Service
Monica Hughes, Rigby Star

True Stories: My Life as a Paramedic (Rapid Response)
Lysa Walder, John Blake Publishing Ltd.

WEBSITES

Read about how to become a paramedic at:
www.nhscareers.nhs.uk/explore-by-career/allied-health-professions/careers-in-the-allied-health-professions/paramedic/entry-and-training/

Learn all about paramedics with these fun games and puzzles at:
www.londonambulance.nhs.uk/getting_involved/schools/games_and_activities.aspx

Watch a video of paramedics talking about their jobs at:
https://learnenglish.britishcouncil.org/en/word-street/paramedics

Note to parents and teachers
Every effort has been made by the Publisher to ensure that these websites contain no inappropriate or offensive material. However, because of the nature of the Internet, it is impossible to guarantee that the contents of these sites will not be altered. We strongly advise that Internet access is supervised by a responsible adult.

INDEX